The analyze of

The Great Gatsby

by

Soulef Larbi Chaht

This year 2021 we celebrate Scott Fitzgerald's masterpiece "the great gatsby" as one of the books that enter the US public domain

The Great Gatsby setting Map

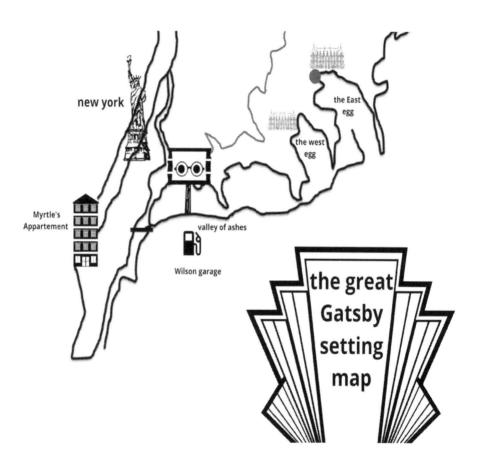

new york

the East egg

the west egg

Myrtle's Appartement

valley of ashes

Wilson garage

the great Gatsby setting map

CHAPTER 1

As we all know, the great Gatsby is narrated by the character Nick Carroway, a humble good man who went new York city looking for a career in stocks after finishing his duty as a soldier in the first world war. Scott Fitzgerald's told us the story of the Great Gatsby using the first person pronoun "I" which present Nick, that is mean that the whole story is told from his vision and his point of view, we are reading what was in Nick's mind, Nick is the structure of the book.

Besides that, nick is an involved character in the story, as readers, we need to take into consideration that his way of seeing things, judging them, evaluating them is not necessarily ours, and we can't consider him the only main character or the hero, because Jay Gatsby is an event maker character as much as Nick, it is a dual hero story.

The flashback used by the writer reflects Nick's education, once he returned from the East, Nick tried to define the experience that he had for himself.

Maybe because he saw in Gatsby a cloud of foul dust, an illusion of success, a perfect dream but not a reality, sometimes he despises Jay for his vulgar ambitions and his way of progressing but he pitied his all energy and gifts and time that was spent wrongly to the wrong person.

Gatsby is the main character of Nick's story, he is a man who attempts to build his wealth empire, he idolizes money, the money for him is something holly, it is the key to enter the rich magic mystic world of eternal happiness and the material success, he wanted to make from money a spiritual ideal, he is a pilgrim to Daisy's heart, but is Daisy's heart is holy and pure?

This is exactly what destroyed him in the end.

Fitzgerald women

Daisy is Tom's wife, Jay's ex-girlfriend, Nick new friend, she is the illusion In the story, the dust that makes Jay blind

Daisy and Jordan are introduced as cold women, maybe graceful, beautiful, romantics but very childish and materialists, and sometimes annoying. It could be the writer's point of view about American women's behavior in that era.

Jordan Bicker: Daisy's friend, a professional golf player, who had a short relationship with Nick Carroway, Day's cousin.

Myrtle

Like the Wasteland citizens, Myrtle is the definition of ironic romance, destructive love, she is the perfect example of the American dream chaser, she wants the rich man with the suit.

The theme of the surface without substance is used almost in all the elements of the story, even in the women characters, beautiful body with empty true feeling.

For example, at the beginning of the story, Nick says that Gatsby's life was an "unbroken series of successful gestures", the word gesture here means that what is introduced perfectly and successfully is hollow from the inside, it is an appearance without emotions.

The story started with Jay looking at the green light coming from the side of the Buchanan mention, Looking at it as an admirer, as a worshiper devoted to something there he believes it, and this what is concluded from his gestures when he stretches his hands to the light.

The first chapter tells us how the 29-year-old Nick Carroway who graduated from Yell, and served in the Army decided to leave the middle west and to live in New York, exactly in a small house in the West Egg near to Jay Gatsby mention, when in the other side in the East egg lives Nick's cousin Daisy, he met Jordan who reveals during dinner to Nick that her husband Tom is having an affair with a lower-class woman in New York.

CHAPTER 2

The second chapter of the book offers us one of the most memorable and important scenes of the story, the billboard face of Doctor T.J.Eckleburg in the "Valley of ashes", all critics and fans agreed that this scene reflected that all that was happening was under God vision, God sees what is happening secretly in this place which is the complete opposite of the first scene-setting of mentions and wealth.

The valley of ashes, a poor area of hard workers miserable people trying to make a living through their ways, even the way is not always moral but they seem as if they hide behind the pretext of poverty.

Through Nick Carroway; the valley of ashes is hell, and he recognizes this reality every time he passes through this gray dusty miserable zone with daisy, the unreal fairy princess of Gatsby.

The color yellow

Scott Fitzgerald uses the color yellow in the landscape of the valley of ashes several times, he reflected daisy through colors, in the buildings around the house of the Wilsons where Tom's mistress lives, in the doctor Eckleburg's spectacles, and it exist also around Gatsby, his clothes, his car, so yellow is a symbol of the purity that can be poison.

Mrs. Wilson is a consumer as much as Tom, they use their desires to get what they want without caring, breaking in their way the human being feelings.

Mr. George Wilson is used as a destruction tool, in the end, this tool will make an end to the illusions of Gatsby dreams, what's ironic is that Mr.George shares with Gatsby the same impulse and appetite, the impulse of George and his extremely powerful love for his wife turned him to an unstoppable killing machine, like Gatsby with his strong love to Daisy made him an unstoppable money machine.

Fitzgerald men

Wilson and Jay share the same stupidity that idolizes what they call "love", and this is what Tom calls "dumb", but they have something the others don't have, maybe this is the reason why they ended up tragically, they have the quality of "humanity", while the others are following the easy choice of money, desire, and comfort.

Jay Gatsby is a man who wants to live the American dream through his huge mention and parties and luxury clothes, but he built all those things on cotton ground.

Tom is daisy's husband, a rich man by inheritance, he sees money as a toy, he grew up playing with this toy over and over, the money is around him, for him and from him, he doesn't chase money, but he uses it when he needs a woman or a car or a horse or a mention.

Nick represents the opposite of this dream, he is a man of reality, he deserves the narrator character because he is out of the dreams and the desires that smash on their way the naive people.

During the chapter, Myrthe joined Tom and nick on the train to New York where she buys a poppy after meeting her sister and her friend in Tom's apartment, while having fun inside, Mythle treats the poor animal with carelessness, it obvious that the poppy means nothing for her, and he bought him just to show off and try to look like an upper-class woman, she couldn't stop mentioning Daisy in her talking finally Tom beats her to make her wake up and to remember that she will never be an upper-class woman.

Chapter 3

Gatsby's parties take a wide place in this chapter, we notice that the use of Jay's character is not a reflection of himself but he is the pathetic optimism of the American dream, the illusion theme take place.

The crates of the fruits, the cars full of people reflect the renewable unlimited consumption of society, no production, only consuming.

The strangers at the party without any reason, just an image of crowded life, but it is an empty sensation, Jay couldn't feel the meaning of magisterial busy life with luxurious parties and rich friends and beautiful sincere love.

"a regular Belasco"

This is what **Owl Eyes** called Gatsby when he met nick in the library, what Owl Eyes meant is that he knows Gatsby just as a spectator knows an actor in a lavish set from David Belasco works, he knows him through his parties, his mention, his genius books that weren't open yet.

Gatsby's smile

Gatsby's smile is one aspect of the theatrical scene that plays every night on his stage which is his mention, he knows exactly how to smile to make the scene dreamy to his unknown visitors who love to be there just for parties.

Jordan and Nick Carroway

Unlike Gatsby's modern world of materials and moral expediency, Nick's world is real and based on honesty and moral firmness, Jordan sees in him the man that can catch her anytime she falls, for her, his presence is just a calculation among many, she is one of the twenty's girls who can offer a short love if they want to, and they leave when they want to.

Nick's infatuation toward Jordan's charm will not make him lose his soundness, he is the observer, the narrator who is protected by his moral traditions.

The chapter is about the parties and the beginning of rumors about Gatsby's source of money, also about Nick's life, Nicks talked about how hard he worked during the summer and how to he dated several women to find the one, and he shows his good intentions toward Jordan that despite her dishonesty could be the one for him.

Chapter 4

Illusion makes him fragile

Gatsby's car plays an important role in this chapter when he arrives with his gorgeous car at Nick's house, he shows his material success once again, he brings with him other sign of the American dream's aspects.

We notice Gatsby's respect and devotion to his materialism, he falls into the trap of idolizing things and people instead of principles and morals what makes him end up in self-destruction.

Scott Fitzgerald used a series of captives adjectives to describe the car to explain how this material thing fascinates Gatsby.

Gatsby's self-illusion doesn't mean that he is laying to people around him, he started to believe that he is the rich powerful Jay Gatsby who daisy still loves and that she will leave her husband for him because he is the American dream successful man to all the women, Gatsby hypnotized himself

What makes an illusion becomes true, is to find a suitable environment to believe in it, the perfect setting, the characters, that is why he made his big parties, to confirm his illusion.

All the fake identities base on illusion and the consequence for that is having a personal emptiness, and if this identity faces a real feeling or a real situation it may collapse suddenly in a tragic way.

Gatsby and Daisy's love

Daisy is the major dream of gatsby's dream list, she is the wheel that makes all his material success grows up, she is the fairy woman that makes his life perfect, ironically her character is as fake as the other elements of gatsby's idols, and just like them all she is a destroys him at the end, Fitzgerald wanted to illustrate the relationship between money and beauty in the American society during the twenties.

In this chapter, Nicks is always a member of Gatsby's parties guests, and his relationship with Jay becomes a friendship, he even meets Meyer Wolfsheim, who has a questionable past of gambling and illegal activities.

In the same chapter, Jay meets Tom, and Jordan told Nick the passionate love story between Jay and Daisy and how her parents refused him for his poverty and social class, this is the motive of Gatsby to becomes a rich man.

CHAPTER 5

Gatsby's appreciation or gratitude to Nicks makes him offer to him a stock deal what nicks declines without any doubt.

Maybe Gatsby was honest or he really wanted to win and conserve his friendship with nick but his way reflects once again that he has nothing to offer but materials, just like he does with Daisy, but Nick is not Daisy or Myrtle, for people like Nick who grew up in the Midwest still have human dignity and real feeling, buy or selling a relationship doesn't exist.

Nick is an honest character, he can tell Jay what he thinks about him, at first he felt some compassion toward him, then he told him what he sees in him, a childish man

"you're acting like a little boy"

Gatsby's shirts

We talked previously about Jay Gatsby material idols, such as the expensive parties and the car, in this chapter, another material satisfaction appears which is the shirts, unlike the others those shirts are not important for what they are but for what they represent, for Tom, for example, a shirt is a shirt, a piece of fabric he can get whenever he wants, but for Jay is is a meaning of elegance and power that makes people impressed, and they are not given to anyone, they are sacred objects that he preserves with care on the big closet, we see his proud of it when he piles the rainbow of the colorful silk of shirt from a higher place over daisy, then she starts to moaning just like a pure soul after praying.

We feel that Gatsby returned to a confident man after watching Daisy's reaction, finally, he got her, and once he gets what he wants, it returns to new material property and for Nick is a loss for Daisy, she just lost her precious place in Jay's dream list.

In this chapter the famous date takes place after Nick arranged a tea meeting between the two "lovers", Jay's behavior shows that he was nervous and excited, when Daisy arrives, nick's house turned into an interior garden full of flowers, he looked more nervous than ever, he even broke Nick's clock but when Nick left them alone, everything turned to normal, even better, it was if their love was rekindled, after that they went to Jay's mention where shirts scene took place.

CHAPTER 6

The flashback

In this chapter the truth starts to reveal, we will meet James Gatz, the 17years old teenager who dreamed of a new version of himself.

Nick will go back to Jame's past, the poor man who wanted to become a rich man lives the American dream literary, Gatz reached his dream and became Jay Gatsby, of course, the character is introduced in a poor fisherman who met a yacht owner whos name is Dane Coody, he hired James as an assistant, James becomes obsessed with luxury, he even changes his name to Jay Gatsby a more fashionable name, after his boss's death, Jay inherited 25,000 dollars from him.

The new money versus the old money

In this chapter, we will notice that Jay did not inherit the real rich men's manners and way of thinking and understanding. The reader notices the difference between a real rich man and a newly rich man when Jay invited three men to dinner and they declined and when they invited him he accepted immediately, while the invitation is just a polite way to thank him for inviting him and not a real invitation to be accepted and here Tom started to feel suspicious about Jay Gatsby.

Also, the writer gives us a new angel of the week relationship between Jay and Daisy during the party. Daisy is in love with the romantic character that Jay is playing more than Jay himself.

Chapter 7

The little toy

Gatsby fired a servant to protect daisy after the rumors, he visits Daisy in her house and he kisses her while Tom is not with them in the living room, at this time her little daughter appears so Daisy sends her back, the girl shows us the ironic relationship between mother and daughter, or let's say a toy, her girl is just another object that makes Daisy's life looks perfect to the others.

The rivals

later Daisy suggests a trip to New York, so the five characters take the cars and go, Jay and Daisy in a car, Nick Jordan and Tom in the second car, Tom becomes more suspicious than ever, he sees the love drawing hearts up their heads.

Fitzgerald shows up another ironic image when Tom stops at the gas station and Mr. Wilson told him that his wife is cheating on him, here Tom can't stand the fact that his two women (wife and mistress) are leaving him.

In the New York apartment, Tom confronts Jay, and immediately Jay told him that Daisy is in love with him and never loved him, Daisy said that she did love Tom, at this moment Tom realized that Daisy started to see the truth about Jay's illusions.

Back home, Daisy hit Myrthul with Jay's car, when Nick goes to jay house he found him hiding between the shrubberies. And he tells him that was Daisy's fault and he is protecting her by not saying anything, here Nick feels disgusted by this inhuman behavior of those rich people who left Myrtle dead on the road.

Myrtle's death reveals two realities, the first one is Daisy's selfishness and her love for money is more brutal than Jay's love of materialism, he wanted the money to have a good status and a love that he always wanted while Daisy's love for money was more than anything, she even uses her youth love to keep her husband for her.

The second reality is that Gatsby remained under the fatal reality that Daisy is his girl, her character looks so familiar to me as a reader because I've seen such a personage in Skyler White in breaking bad.

This chapter reverses everything, we discover the true intention of Daisy who used Jay to win back her husband Tom who was cheating on her with Myrtle, the illusions of Jay disappears, and all that he did for her full apart.

Chapter 8

After the bad night of Myrtle's death, Nick visited Gatsby and he encouraged him to leave the West Egg for a while.

Gatsby told Nick his love story with Daisy before the war w and how the love night made him feels that Daisy was his wife and how she promised to wait for him till he comes back from the war, but Daisy met Tom in the following spring and she found on him what she needs as a girl from the upper class.

Meanwhile, Mr. Wilson was crying his dead wife despite her betrail, he was convinced that he needed to revenge her death and he told Tom what he thought, Tom was glad to tell him that Jay's car kills his wife, George went to Jay's house where he found him in the swimming pool, he killed him with a gan than he killed himself, Jay's body was discovered by Nick after he didn't answer his calls, Nick was so shocked, he even cut his relationship with Jordan feeling pity about his friend Jay.

Daisy continued her life as if nothing happened or nobody was dead

Chapter 9

In this chapter Gatsby's funeral is empty of people, no friends appeared that day, only Nick, Jay's father, and few servants, Nicks was surprised how Mr. Henry C. Gatz talked so nice about his son insisting about the fact that his son could be a great man, although he abanded everything from his past even his father, chasing for more money and dreams, Nick also meet Tom and he told him about Jay's so Tom express his sadness because he can't go to his apartment new York again, this made Nick more disgusted!

The Buchanans and all the inhabitants of Westland can express only the carelessness that comes with wealth, the egotism of moral primitives, all they can do is to smash things up letting the poor people cleaning their mess.

Nick Carroway prepared himself to go back to the Midwest, in his last night, he visited Jay's house for the last time then he left all those pathetic charaters and tragic scenes behind him.

Symbols

The green light cames from Buchanan's mention, generally, The green color in literature is a symbol of money, also it is a symbol of the American dream this shown where Gatsby tries to touch is with his hand

The valley of ashes: means "the left behind" of the rich people, and the perfect example is Mrs. and Ms. Wilson who was died at the end of the story after being two tools for the rich people, a tool of desire and a tool of revenge.

The broken clock is a small symbol but very meaningful, it is an indication of the "too late" for Jay and Daisy's love when they met in Nick's house to revive their love.

DR Eckerlburg eyes is a symbol of the immorality of the society in the roaring twenties, the American society abanded her religion to replace it with satisfying desires

Themes

Classes

The geography in the story is very important, we discover many places such as the East Egg that represents the elite society the owners of the old money, on the other hand, we discover the West Egg the society of the new money while the Valley of ashes represents the middle and lower class.

Superficiality versus the truth

Jay Gatsby changed his name and he created a false past to make his image bright and his status higher, we can see a real past and a superficial present that lead to a tragic end, chasing the American dream is a major theme in the story, everyone is chasing money and a good place in society.

Degradation of society

Scot Fitzgerald wrote this book before the great depression, but he had a very clear vision of the bad causes it, the carless society and the wast of money in superficial thing, the illegal ways to earn money, all these are factors that indicate the fall of the social values and economy.

Main Characters

Nick Carroway:

the narrator of the novel is the traditional moral codes of American society, at first, we notice that he was amazed by the shinning world of riches, the mentions, the luxurious cars, the parties, the beautiful girls but in the end he understands the emptiness of this world, he is a man that knows the values of human relationships such as the true love, we see that he looks for his future woman and his intentions toward Jordan are honest even in the end of their relationship we discover that the motive the break up is not cheating, he realized that Jordan is not a woman that shares him the moral values which they are the basics of life for him

Also in his friendship with Jay, he was a true friend, he gave him pieces of advice, he was there for him when he wanted to see his lover, he was one of the rare people who attended his funeral.

Jay Gatsby

The main character in the novel, and at the same time a symbolic character, is the symbol of Idealism that is made from materialism,

He is a pathetic dreamer who sacrificed himself in the name of illusionary love, he considered that material success as a major rite among the spiritual rites to make an identity, he believed that he can recreate the reality through his will, he chased Daisy not as a woman, but as an idol, as the perfection of love.

We feel some honesty despite his fake life, wealth, and gestures, he is honest in his big desire to have Daisy as a wife, he wanted her so bad and protected her even when she killed a human, but he dropped into the swamp of devoting and worshiping the materials standards.

Daisy Buchanan

The girls who swing between Tom and Jay, a beautiful woman with cold emotions, chasing her comfort, using people to reach satisfaction of an upper-class woman, for Scott Fitzgerald, she is the perfect model of the roaring twenties material women who anded the values of religion and morals for a loud life of parities and Jazz music.

The writer admitted that daisy was beautiful and physically attractive but he explained that she is also one of those women who can be dangerous and destructive machines.

Daisy doesn't have the essentials, she empty from the inside, and Jay can fill this emptiness with his illusionary pictures of romance and success.

Tom Buchanan

Daisy's brutal husband who run after his desires, the lover of Myrtle Wilson, is the symbol of the Wasteland rulers, a rich careless rude man with no spiritual values, once he makes a mess he uses other people to clean up for him

He is a cold man with no feelings, he cheated on his wife and he even introduced his lover to his wife's cousin also we see this coldness after Myrtle death when he said to Tom that he can't go to the New York apartment anymore, also he is a week man, he slapped Myrtle, and he used his chocked husband to take revenge on his enemy Jay.

Jordan Baker

Anther copy of daisy, beautiful, especially on white dresses, a good golf player, she likes to party, an opportunist woman who looks for her self-satisfying, a typical example of Wasteland rulers.

Myrtle Wilson

The fleshly greedy woman who cheats on her husband, a vulgar woman who wanted to reach the upper-class status, another parasite woman dies violently just like she lives, full of blood.

George Wilson

An honest poor man who works in is a garage in a tuff environment, he truly loved his wife, this love costs him his life, at the end he kills Jay Gatsby thinking that he was the driver of the car who killed his wife then he kills himself.

Pammy

Tom and Daisy's daughter, appeared for a very short time in the living room scene to interrupt her mother love moment with her lover. Daisy called her "dream" because she completes her mother's collection of a rich woman's property.

Mr. Henry Gatz

Jay's father, in other words, Jame's father, appears in Jay's funeral to show Nick the pathetic notes from James's diaries when he was young as if he wanted to explain to Nick that his son could be a good man.

F. Scott Fitzgerald

was born in St. Paul, Minnesota, to a well-off upper-middle-class family, his masterwork was made as movie four times, he writes about a man who invents himself to achieve his dream, he never writes about himself, yet he reflected parts of his on his works, he worked in the army, he wrote about youth and his generation, Zelda was his golden girl, yet she was rich for him, hard to obtain, after the war he worked in New York, he kept writing despite the previous declines of his work, finally, his work was accepted, and Zelda also decided to accept him and they got married in 1920, their relationship was full of parties, just like Gatsby dreams, they had a little girl just like Pammy, a lot of literary critics says that the characters of his books are very similar to him and his environment.

Printed in Great Britain
by Amazon